IMAGES
of America

WHITE
MOUNTAIN
HOTELS, INNS, AND TAVERNS

IMAGES
of America

WHITE MOUNTAIN
HOTELS, INNS, AND TAVERNS

David Emerson

ARCADIA

First published 1996
Copyright © David Emerson, 1996

ISBN 0-7524-0289-7

Published by Arcadia Publishing,
an imprint of the Chalford Publishing Corporation
One Washington Center, Dover, New Hampshire 03820
Printed in Great Britain

With special thanks to the Conway Public Library,
the Conway Historical Society,
and Janet Hounsell.

Contents

Introduction

The saga of hotels, inns, and taverns is integral to the history of New Hampshire's White Mountains. Early settlers were quick to realize the potential value of offering lodging to teamsters, explorers, and naturalists. As the region's fame spread, businessmen and prosperous farmers began to visit the mountains. When travel to the "Crystal Hills" became easier, the area blossomed into a playground of the well-to-do.

It is hard to imagine the White Mountains of the grand hotel age, when families brought trunks and servants with them when they traveled, and ladies changed dresses five times each day. The rich competed with one another in outrageous bouts of ostentation.

Like the grandeur (and decadence) of Rome, the golden era of the White Mountains could not last. America was restless. With the country's love affair with the automobile in full swing, overnight cabins began to edge out the hotels. Cabins evolved into motels. There was no longer a niche for the huge hostelries. Like great shadowy ghosts of dowager empresses, the grand buildings stood silent and alone, anachronisms in an unfamiliar world. The more fortunate of the great edifices perished swiftly on mammoth pyres of flame, avoiding the indignity of rot and neglect. A very few survived as relics of grander days. The inns fared better, surviving as boarding houses, ski lodges, and eventually, bed and breakfasts.

Fortunately for us, photography developed in time to record many of the White Mountain's hotels, inns, and taverns in their heyday. The black-and-white images that follow contain glimpses of the most majestic era of one of the most beautiful regions in the United States.

One
By the Side of the Road

The first White Mountain hostelries were taverns and farmhouses. Taverns, strategically placed on stage routes, offered lodging to dust-weary travelers. Accommodations were not always luxurious; passengers were at the mercy of the stage companies. Travel was an adventure—not for the the squeamish or weak of heart.

A few farmers, with a spark of entrepreneurialism, began to open their homes to strangers. Hayes and Dolly Copp offered hospitality, solid country food, and commodious shelter to those hardy enough to visit the Crawford wilderness.

North Conway's Samuel Thompson, realizing the potential of visiting artists, offered special rates to painters. Illustrations of the spectacular mountain scenery served to attract increasingly larger numbers of visitors. The White Mountains were on their way to becoming a resort destination.

Simple farmhouses, like the one pictured here, were the forerunners of the resort hotels. As well as attracting hardy settlers, the mountains were a magnet to naturalists, artists, and explorers. Farm families were happy to provide accommodations in exchange for a few pennies and news from the outside world.

589

The first building on this site was erected in 1792. From its earliest beginnings, it served as a stopping place for travelers through Crawford Notch. In 1823, Ethan Crawford agreed to provision it for those trekking through the wilderness, but the logistics of hauling in supplies soon made the enterprise unfeasible. Later that year, Samuel Willey Jr. moved his family into the house and continued to supply lodging for travelers. In 1826, a landslide killed the Willey family and hired help, all of whom had taken shelter a short distance from the building. Ironically, the house remained intact. Famed hotel man Horace Fabyan repaired the house in 1884, adding a two-and-one-half-story hotel. The original Willey House burned in September 1899.

Although Eleazar Rosebrook is sometimes credited with opening the region's first inn around 1803, Andrew McMillan was operating a hostelry in North Conway by 1784. The venerable hotel, which stood on the site now occupied by Gralyn Antiques, was noted for grand views of the Saco Intervales. It was destroyed by fire in September 1899.

A contemporary newspaper account described the McMillan House fire: "A Miss Rogers of Portland was awakened by the smell of smoke and at once gave the alarm. Clerk Brook, who slept in a room directly beneath her, heard the first cry and immediately rushed upstairs and aroused the guests and servants. He then started for the village and gave the alarm. Before assistance could arrive, the house was a mass of flames, and but a small amount of furniture was saved."

Lucy and Danforth Atherton were the first in the Goshen section of Conway to open up their home to summer boarders. One of the earliest guests at the Atherton Farm was Louisa May Alcott, who wrote much of *Eight Cousins* there.

Dr. Samuel Bemis completed this granite structure in 1860. Much of the stone was quarried from the Sawyer River. The doctor—a noted (and rather eccentric) dentist, as well as a pioneer photographer—died in 1881, bequeathing the house to George M. Morey. In 1920 the Morey family opened the twenty-six-room mansion to paying guests, first as the NotchLand Inn, and later as the Inn Unique.

Ormand Merrill used the money he received when he mustered out from Civil War duty to renovate this Conway Village farm into an inn. The much-expanded building continues to serve as a resort.

Early taverns served as stage stops, hostelries, and centers of community life. Smith's Tavern in Intervale is shown here.

Like many others, Jim and Addie Annis opened their Albany farm to hunters, trappers, and tourists. Jim subsidized the inn by driving stages, delivering mail, and breaking horses. The Annis farm was located at the end of the Bear Notch Road near what is now the Kancamagus Highway.

Shelburne's Philbrick Farm, which is noted as the oldest inn in the United States to be operated by the same family at the same site, was opened to guests in 1861. The first guests were two Harvard students who, lingering too late on a fishing expedition, were caught by darkness and obliged to seek shelter with the Philbrick family. Their glowing reports of the family's hospitality began a long tradition at the farm.

The Pleasant View in Franconia was a typical resort farm. Guests could experience country life while enjoying spectacular mountain views. Innkeepers were not particularly creative when it came to naming their inns: Pleasant Views were found in New London, Sutton, Antrim, Bennington, and Pelham; Pleasant View Farms in Belmont, Brookfield, Effingham, Freedom, Danbury, Dunbarton, and Warner; and Pleasant View Houses in Gilmanton, Bradford, Bennington, and Monroe.

Rural scenes, like this of a shady lane leading to the Mountain Park House, were a treat to those used to the bustle, dust, and heat of eastern cities.

Like many White Mountain inns, Center Villa began as a farmhouse. James Willey built the original part of this North Conway landmark in about 1820. By 1892, the Litchfield family was running it as the Center Villa Hotel. Fred Eastman, son of Eastman Hotel owner Alfred Eastman, ran the Villa throughout the first part of the twentieth century. Harvey Dow Gibson bought the building during the 1930s for use, in conjunction with Birchmont, as a retreat for employees of the Manufacturer's Trust. The Center Villa currently houses offices.

Two

The Mountains Come of Age

During the early decades of the nineteenth century, travel to the White Mountains was by stage and steamship. Roads, choked with dust or clogged with mud, made journeys difficult and uncomfortable. The arrival of the railroad changed the White Mountains forever.

Rail travel was swift and pleasurable and made the supplies needed to maintain large hotels readily available. Prominent businessmen began to send their families to the mountains to escape the heat, disease, and chaos of the city. Trains allowed the well-to-do to bring their baggage and servants and to settle in for weeks or months. Rough and tumble country inns evolved into genteel resorts catering to the rich and famous. It was a new era for the White Mountains.

During the mid-nineteenth century, rail travel was the standard means of transportation. It is not surprising that trains were chosen as a means of carrying visitors to the summit of Mount Washington. Invented by Sylvester Marsh of Littleton, the Cog Railway was completed in 1869. A 6-mile line connected the Cog with the Fabyan House.

White Mts. N.H., Crawford House and Gateway.

The arrival of the railroad signaled the beginning of a building frenzy in the White Mountains. Guests arrived by rail-car loads while hostelries grew to accommodate them. Hotels were built with access to the railroad in mind and stations were situated with the hotels in mind. Many hotel advertisements included "free carriages to the station," even when the station was only a few hundred feet distant.

By 1828, traffic through Crawford Notch had increased enough to warrant a small hotel and livery. Abel Crawford, for whom the notch was named, along with his son, Ethan Allen Crawford, erected a 120-by-36-foot building known as the Notch House. Part of the attraction of the notch was the Willey House, made notable by the infamous 1826 slide. Henry David Thoreau was a Notch House guest in 1839. The Notch House was the predecessor of two Crawford Houses. The second Crawford House is shown here.

The Kearsarge House (on the left with the flag) and Kearsarge Hall (on the right behind the Kearsarge School for Boys) were owned and managed by North Conway hotel men S.W. and S.D. Thompson. The smaller building on the left is Valley Inn, part of the Kearsarge House complex. The hotels had a combined capacity of three hundred guests. Transient rates ran form $3.00 to $3.50 per day while regular board ranged from $10 to $21 per week.

Main Street Bethlehem was lined with grand hotels fronted by expansive verandas. During the height of the hotel era, Bethlehem could claim thirty hostelries. Dozens of coaches waited at the station for the arrival of the "city people." Most of the hotels opened around July 1. Some of the hotel men traveled to the Carolinas, Georgia, and Florida in the winter, taking staff members with them.

Although not always thought of in terms of being a White Mountain town, Bethel, Maine, has had a long association with the mountains. Part of Bethel's attraction was its proximity to popular attractions including the Albany Basins, Rumford and Screw-auger Falls, Sunrise Rock, and Paradise Hill.

22

White Mountain poet Starr King said of Lancaster: "There is no single meadow view of Lancaster equal to the Intervale at North Conway. But the river is incomparably superior to the Saco; and the combined charm for walks or rides, of meadow and river—the charm not of wildness such as the darker and more rapid Androscoggin gives, but a cheerful brightness and beneficence—Lancaster is unrivaled." The most prominent Lancaster hotels were the Lancaster House, the Williams House, and the American Hotel.

In 1887, the Lake Winnepesaukee "navy" consisted of the *Mount Washington*, the *Lady of the Lake*, several smaller excursion boats, a few fresh water yachts, and a flotilla of rowboats. This view is from the Elmwood, one of more than forty Wolfeboro hotels and boarding houses.

The proprietors of Bethlehem's thirty hotels engaged in friendly competition for guests. Arrivals who boarded the wrong wagon at the busy station sometimes stayed in the wrong hotel for several days before discovering their mistake. The hotel men considered it a great coup to steal another establishment's clientele in this manner.

A Boston & Maine Railroad publication said of Whitefield: "This little community remained but half awake during the first half century of its existence, but with the advent of the railroads, it began to take a different view of life . . . Whitefield has grown to be one of the most thriving towns in New Hampshire."

Almost all the hotels kept "tallyhos" to ferry guests to and from the station, carry them on drives to local landmarks, and to compete with other establishments in lavish coaching parades. These conveyances were manufactured by Abbott and Downing, makers of the Concord Coach.

Built in 1869 by Joshua Trickey, the Thorne Mountain House become Wentworth Hall under the proprietorship of Trickey's son-in-law, Marshall Wentworth. The Wentworths added several large cottages during the 1880s and built a stone castle as their private residence. Wentworth Hall raised most of the food served in its dining room and enjoyed its own power plant located at Jackson Falls. Besides this pasteurizing plant, Jackson's Wentworth Hall operated greenhouses, a large laundry, a blacksmith shop, a print shop, a boutique, a casino, a telegraph office, and a golf course. The stables housed up to sixty horses.

Opened in 1905, the second Profile House was described as "One of the most beautiful resort hotels in the country where only the best can be obtained," with "Every comfort and luxury known to hotel keeping." Sensing the importance of the automobile, but unaware of its far-reaching effect on the industry, the Profile House also advertised "Fine roads and every convenience for automobile parties." Twenty-nine cottages, each with up to seventeen rooms, were connected by covered walkways to the four hundred-room third Profile House. The first Profile House is shown here.

Before steam heating became commonplace, few of the larger hotels remained open in winter. The ever-present danger of fire combined with the logistics of heating several hundred rooms made winter openings impractical. The Profile House is shown here.

Around 1850, Notch House proprietor Thomas Crawford (brother of Ethan) began construction of the Crawford House. The Crawfords had lured tourists to "The Great Notch" by providing a bridal path to the top of Mount Washington. After financial woes began to afflict Thomas, the unfinished hotel was sold to Ebenezer Eastman. Eastman's untimely death in 1853 left the completion of the building in the hands of a group of businessmen from Haverhill and Littleton. The hotel shown here was built after fire destroyed the first Crawford House in 1859. The remaining shell of the abandoned second Crawford House became, itself, a victim of fire in 1977.

The Mountain Park House provided up to forty guests with a trout stream "a stone's throw from the hotel." Farm resorts of this type dotted the New Hampshire countryside.

Named for Horace Fabyan, the most famous of the White Mountain hotel men, the second Fabyan House was completed in 1873 at a cost of $150,000. There was great controversy generated by the leveling of the landmark "Giant's Grave" to provide a site for the hotel. The Fabyan House was a central point where White Mountain rail lines converged.

The Flume House in Franconia Notch was christened for the popular attraction of the same name. Note the line of carriages gathered in this Heywood stereograph. Besides providing family entertainment during the days before television and radio, stereographs were also an important means of advertising the virtues of the White Mountains.

The Bretton Arms was once used to house the chauffeurs of those visiting the Mount Washington Hotel. It has since been renovated into guest rooms.

Eagle Cliffs and Eagle Peaks can be found throughout the region. At least ten different hostelries included "eagle" in their names. This winter stereograph shows Eagle Cliff in Franconia Notch.

A Hallworth postcard view of the Russell House in North Woodstock displays the growth of a small White Mountain inn. Note the large addition to the original twenty-guest farmhouse.

The first Profile House, shown above, encompassed 11,000 acres including the Old Man of the Mountains. After the third Profile House burned, the site became a state park.

The Mountain View House in Whitefield treated 125 guests at a time to views of Franconia Notch. For those seeking more activity, proprietors William. F. Dodge and son offered an excellent golf course. The above photograph was taken from the hotel grounds.

Once known for the manufacture of iron, Franconia's convenient location and sweeping panoramas soon made it an ideal tourist destination. This is the view from Sugar Hill.

The Kearsarge House in North Conway began as a simple farm. It was enlarged four times, becoming one of the largest and most popular of the East Side hotels. The evenly-spaced pines that shaded the boardwalk to the station can still be seen today. When the massive structure burned in 1917, an estimated one thousand people turned out to watch.

Many of the larger hotels maintained bands. The Kearsarge House band is shown here. Weekly "hops" provided an opportunity for Victorian ladies to display their finery. One visitor reportedly brought forty-nine dresses with her. The North Conway Station can been seen on the right.

Lady Blanche Murphy, British expatriate and North Conway resident, was bemused by the tendency to gossip and snipe, so evident on the wide hotel verandas. She was also quite shocked by the visitors' casual attitude concerning the rights and feelings of the locals. The Kearsarge House porch is depicted in this photograph.

Not built until the turn of the century, the Fairview in Intervale supplied many modern conveniences for the reasonable rate of $1.50 to $2.00 per day. The sixty-five-guest hotel was located across from the entrance to Intervale Park, a celebrated religious retreat.

The Intervale House in Lower Bartlett was built by William Trickey in 1860. Stephen Mudgett later ran the hotel, which offered panoramic views of the Saco River. A golf course was established on the nearby intervals. J.D. Rockefeller Sr. was a frequent guest.

By 1902, two of Littleton's hotels, the Thayer (shown here) and the Northern, had been consolidated under one management. It was stated by the proprietor, W.S. Dunham, that advantages to summer visitors and the traveling public were trebled by the new arrangement. Chisholm's *White Mountain Guide* (1887) declared that Littleton could have become a premier resort village if only its inhabitants had chosen to retain the original name of Chiswick. Chisholm considered the name Littleton too mundane to attract tourists.

In 1902, proprietor J.M. Mathes advertised special June, July, and September rates at the Mount Agassiz in Bethlehem. The hotel offered electric lights, bathrooms, and open fires to forty guests. Some hotels charged guests 25¢ to use the one bathroom located on each floor.

Mountain teams were a specialty of the Ravine House in Randolph, located on the north side of "the Great Range." Their advertisements enticed guests with the promise of fine drives and beautiful walks.

North Woodstock presented a majestic 25 mile vista of the Pemigewasset Valley with access to many popular White Mountain attractions. The Mount Adams House hosted many of the three thousand annual visitors to the community.

During the heyday of the hotel era, Jefferson boasted nineteen hotels. The Starr King, named in honor of the White Mountain poet, Thomas Starr King, and the Waumbek are shown in this photograph. The original Waumbek, built in 1860, housed 450 guests. It was further enlarged at the turn of the century. The majestic Waumbek burned in 1928.

Lake Winnepesaukee offered some of the first White Mountain views to those headed north from New York and Boston. Before the railroad was extended, passengers crossed the lake by steamship, then continued north by stage. The Hotel Weirs enjoyed both lake and mountain vistas.

White Mountains, N. H., The Sinclair House, Bethlehem

The Sinclair House, which graced Bethlehem's Main Street, was built in 1865 by John Sinclair. Mr. Sinclair ran for governor three times and for the U.S. Senate in 1876.

The 2,000-foot elevation of the Look-Off in Sugar Hill provided spectacular views as well as "Perfect exemption from hay fever." A farm was added in 1891, supplying milk and vegetables to the hotel. By 1902, other bonuses included: electric lights in every room, a telephone and telegraph, and an elevator. Iron fire escapes were provided for each floor.

The original Mount Pleasant House, built in 1876, was a blocky, unassuming, 120-by-40-foot building. The hotel was enlarged in 1881 and again in 1895, eventually becoming one of the premier White Mountain hostelries. In 1896, a plan was unveiled to create a lawn stretching from the hotel to the base of Mount Washington. The scheme was later abandoned. Early in the nineteenth century, the Mount Pleasant and the Mount Washington were run as companion hotels. The Mount Pleasant was razed in 1939.

The Maplewood, one of the most spectacular of the White Mountain hotels, included a 500 acre farm, 18-hole golf course, maple orchard, and outstanding stable. Located in Bethlehem, the two hundred-room Maplewood burned in January 1963.

Opened in 1889, the Maplewood Casino boasted a dance floor, bowling alleys, and a golf course. The Casino fast became a popular Bethlehem social center, and was the site of an annual gala ball as well as many other important events. It was completely renovated in 1988.

Always recognizable by its distinctive tower, Russell Cottages remained in the Russell family until the 1950s. Part of the complex now houses a ski club.

At the turn of the century, golf was all the rage in the White Mountains. Most of the larger hotels provided links. The putting green at Russell Cottages is shown here.

In 1863 Willard Russell and his son Frank opened their Kearsarge Village farm to guests. Joined by another son, Henry, they added the Eastman farm, the annex, and Merrill Cottage. Russell Cottages could accommodate 120 guests. In 1892, when this photograph was taken, rates ran from $7 to $12, typical for smaller hotels. The nearby Kearsarge House charged $25 for its best rooms.

This 1891 B.W. Kilburn stereograph, entitled *Bright as Day*, extols the winter beauty of the White Mountains. The Littleton-based Kilburn studio churned out thousands of stereographs, helping to publicize the area's virtues.

The fifty-guest Moat View house advertised 300 feet of piazza overlooking the Moat Mountains. Like many hotels, this Kearsarge inn offered freedom from "Rose colds" and hay fever.

Alfred Eastman began taking in boarders in his North Conway home in 1867. As the number of guests outgrew the capacity of the house, a large addition was built, connected to the original house by a dining room ell. In later years, Alfred's son Harry carried on the business.

In 1917, fire erupted in the kitchen wing of the Hotel Eastman, worked its way through the dining room ell, and eventually destroyed the main wing of the building. Although three-quarters of the furniture was saved, almost all of the china, linen, and silverware was lost. Each hotel had its own china pattern, usually with the establishment's name emblazoned upon it.

Samuel Thoms, Hiram Abbott, and Captain Nathaniel Abbott built the Conway House in 1850 as the centerpiece of the stage lines they managed. Noted guests included Mary and Tad Lincoln, Franklin Pierce, Horace Greeley, John Greenleaf Whittier, and "game-eyed" Ben Butler. The frame was built by Jacob Berry, who was responsible for the construction of many covered bridges. The finest materials were used in the fabrication of the building, with costs reaching the then-princely sum of $50,000. During its heyday, it was not unusual for the Conway House to serve dinner to two hundred people. Shortly before it burned in 1912, the structure had been updated with electric lights, telephones, and private baths.

This 1920 photograph shows the gracious and inviting porch of the Presidential Inn.

The Sunset Music Hall, to the right of the Sunset Pavilion, now houses the Eastern Slope Music Theater. The smaller building was spared when a 1940 fire destroyed the hotel. The Pavilion was purchased by Harvey Dow Gibson and annexed to the Eastern Slope Inn.

In 1902, the Oxford House in Fryeburg kept a herd of thirty Jersey cows to supply milk, cream, and butter to its guests. Also offered were electric lights, private baths *en suite*, and pure mineral water from a boiling spring. The mineral water was not abundant enough to quench a fire, which, three years later, began in the hotel and spread along Fryeburg's Main Street.

White Mountain coaching parades probably originated in Bethlehem in 1887. Three years later, North Conway jumped on the band wagon (or Concord Coach) and began East Side parades (in reference to the eastern slope of Mount Washington). The Eastern Slope designation was later replaced with the ubiquitous "Mount Washington Valley." North Side parades began in Lancaster in 1895. The Intervale House coach is shown here in front of the Sinclair House in Bethlehem.

Parades were held in Bethlehem from 1887 until about 1935. Automobiles began to enter the parades around 1911. August 22 was the designated parade day in Bethlehem. This photograph captured crowds enjoying an East Side parade. Up to 20,000 people turned out for the lavish spectacles.

Each hotel entered a coach decorated with its own colors. Usually a hotel guest was chosen to chair the decoration committee. At times, decorators were imported from the city to work their magic. Sometimes several thousand dollars were spent on coaching parade entries, with paper, cloth, and flowers covering the coaches, passengers, and horses. In 1889, P.T. Barnum attended the Bethlehem parade. While the hotel coaches were being festooned, wagons were used to ferry guests to and from the station. Prizes were awarded in several categories, including best team and prettiest passengers. The coach above was entered in an East Side parade by Kearsarge's Ridge Hotel.

Guests disport on the lawn of the Keeley Institute, known alternately as the Artists Falls House and Forest Glen Inn. Note the surrey standing before the inn.

The coaching parades often included domestic wagons drawn by oxen as well as the hotel tallyhos with their magnificent teams. The governor awarded prizes in front of the Kearsarge House in North Conway. This entry is from the Keeley Institute (Forest Glen Inn).

Factory at Lexington,

Boston JUN 28 1902 190

The Kearsarge Hotel Co
to Conway N. H.

TRADE MARKS.

DIAMOND FINISH LAUNDRY STARCH.
LAWSON PINK. MINUTE MAN.
LEXINGTON.

Bought of

THE R. I. SHERMAN MFG. CO

Manufacturers, Canners and Importers.

Terms: 288 & 290 STATE and 117 & 119 COMMERCE STREETS.

All Claims must be made within 10 days of receipt of goods.

CASES	DOZ.								
3	6	**LAWSON PINK,**	Yallow Tomatoes	4.25	12	75	✓
6	12	" " "	Lima Beans	1.25	15	00	✓
6	12	" " "	Refugee "	1.30	15	60	✓
6	12	" " "	Ex Sift Peas	1.75	21	00	✓
3	6	" " "	White Cherries	3.00	18	00	✓
3	6	" " "	L. C. Peaches	2.25	13	50	✓
3	6	" " "	Slic Pine	2.15	12	90	✓
3	3		Yallow Apples	3.60	10	80	✓
					119	55	
		Settled Sept 2 1902	30% Cal		30	00	
		The R. I. Sherman Mfg. Co.			89	55	

The logistics of running a five hundred-guest hotel were overwhelming. Many of the staff members worked in Florida and Georgia hotels during the winter months, returning to the White Mountains in the late spring.

An eight-horse hitch, pausing in front of the Eastman House, demonstrates the circus-like atmosphere that sometimes pervaded the hotel era. Note the daring performer standing on the back of the lead horse. The costume may have been considered even more daring than the feat. The lady on the far right is riding sidesaddle.

NORTH CONWAY HOUSE.

The North Conway House met with a somewhat unusual fate when it was sliced asunder and moved to a side street. It remains today in the form of two separate buildings. The hotel's original grounds are now occupied by the North Conway Public Library.

At Pitman Hall in Bartlett, horses were fully as important as guests. The hotel, justifiably famous for its livery, was the scene of many horse auctions. Pitman Hall advertised: "buckboards, seating from two to twenty, carryalls, surreys, phaetons, village carts, etc., and an elegant tallyho always in readiness for the ever-popular coaching parties."

Coaching parade entries incorporated individual hotel colors as well as rousing cheers. During one parade, riders on the Sinclair House coach used the unique cheer: "With a ve-vo with a vi-vo, with a ve-vo, vi-vo, vum. Get a rat trap bigger than a cat trap, vum. Get a cat trap bigger than a rat trap, vum. Cannibal, Cannibal, zip-boom-bah, Sinclair, Sinclair, Rah-Rah-Rah!" The Kearsarge House can be seen in the background of this East Side parade view.

The picturesque and usually-peaceful village of Fryeburg was the scene of the bloodiest battle ever fought in Maine when Captain Lovewell engaged Chief Paugus. In later days, Fryeburg offered more genteel activities, including trips by horse trolley to the Chataqua Grounds. The Oxford was Fryeburg's largest hostelry.

Not all of the White Mountain inns were dependent on tourists. The Woodlawn in Fryeburg also hosted river drivers.

The Conway House.

THE CONWAY HOUSE is beautifully situated in a delightful village, in full view of the whole range of the White Mountains, near the junction of the Swift and Saco rivers, one-third of a mile from the Conway Station of the Eastern Division, Boston & Maine Railroad. Conway Station, on the Maine Central Railroad, is three miles distant. Special arrangements made to accommodate commercial and other travelers on this line. All modern appliances have been adopted in bath rooms and their appurtnances. Rooms large, and well ventilated, many of them suites of two or three, being admirably arranged for families or parties of friends.

Fine views from all sides of the House.

All interior arrangements were made with reference to the comfort of guests.

The table will be kept up to the high standard of former years.

The Mountain Spring Water used on the table, has long been famed for its health giving properties.

Billiard and Pool Table, and other sources of amusement.

The walks and drives from the house are unexcelled.

Good Livery Stable connected with the House.

For further information, terms, etc., address

L. L. BLOOD & SON,

The Conway House was once run by renowned hotel man Horace Fabyan. A frequent guest was poet John Greenleaf Whittier. Registers from the hotel record many traveling players who performed at the nearby "Conway Opera House."

Photographer Nathan Pease captured this view of the interior of a North Conway souvenir shop. The balsam pillows are emblazoned with the motto: "Fragrant Memories of Bretton Woods."

The Sunset Pavilion,

NORTH CONWAY, N. H.

Open from June 1 to October 20. . . . . . Accommodations for 150 Guests.

M. L. MASON, PROPRIETOR.

This Hotel has a remarkably fine situation, at the northerly end of the village. The lawn is of unusual size and beauty, filling a wide space between the house and the road, and adorned with elm-trees, maples, and balm-of-gileads.

The parlors, office, dining-room, and whole lower story, are very attractive, with light, cheerful furnishings and open fireplace.

The chambers are large and pleasant, and have Electric Bells. There is pure running spring water on each story, and a large Bath Room on the first story.

A wide piazza, more than 300 feet long, affords a charming promenade for the guests.

The Music Room or great Parlor is 60 feet long by 30 feet wide, with polished hard-wood floor, and finished throughout in natural wood. The architecture is unique and beautiful; at the lower end of this room is a huge fireplace, 15 feet high and 10 feet across, with granite coping, brick shelves and wide hearth. The room is connected with the main house by the piazza, westerly to the crest of Sunset Bank, the windows commanding a long stretch of the Intervales of the Saco River.

A fine Orchestra will be in attendance during the season.

A good Livery Stable is connected with the Hotel.

The drainage of the House is perfect. Being located on Sunset Bank, which is of high elevation, guarantees thorough drainage at all times.

A faithful Watchman will be on duty throughout the night.

There are free Hotel Coaches to and from all trains.

✴ ROUTES TO NORTH CONWAY. ✴

From Boston—By Boston and Maine Railroad (and Eastern); two through trains each day. About five hours' ride.

Via Portland—Boston and Maine Railroad to Portland, thence by Maine Central Railroad to North Conway. Two trains daily.

By Boston and Portland Steamship Co. and Maine Central Railroad. One through train daily; close connection at Portland.

Mahlon Mason's Sunset Pavilion vaunted its excellent drainage made possible by its position on "Sunset Bank." In an era when the environment was not a high priority, perfect drainage usually meant a site uphill from the nearest river. The massive hotels dotting the region produced mountains of waste, making higher elevations coveted for more than views.

The Kearsarge House was the largest North Conway hotel, with accommodations for three hundred guests. It was open year-round until 1878 when the operation became seasonal. The Kearsarge's 9-hole links, opened in 1895, later became the core of the North Conway Country Club.

JEFFERY HOUSE,

NORTH CONWAY, N. H.

This home-like House will be open for the accommodation of summer travel on the first day of June, 1891, many improvements having been made since last year. Will accommodate twenty-five guests. Has large open wood fireplaces in all public rooms.

THE JEFFERY HOUSE has one of the best locations of any hotel in North Conway. It stands on a high elevation, where a fine view of all the mountains and intervales can be obtained. It is near the Boston & Maine and Maine Central Railroad stations, and carriages meet all parties if notified.

The farm connected with the House abundantly supplies the table with fresh vegetables, milk, eggs, etc. A beautiful large lawn is on two sides of the House, where a fine tennis court is laid out. The rooms are large, well lighted and well ventilated. The House is supplied with pure spring water through iron pipes. The drainage is first-class, making it a most convenient as well as delightful place to spend the summer vacation. June is the best month for trouting. Terms, $7 to $10 per week.

For further information address the manager,

H. C. JEFFERY,

NORTH CONWAY, N. H.

LOCK BOX NO. 176.

Although one of the smaller White Mountain inns, the Jeffrey House provided many of the same amenities as the more prominent hotels.

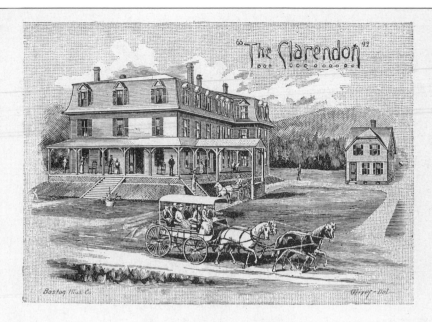

The Clarendon is a new hotel built, in modern style, with open fire-places, etc. It is situated on high ground, and commands an extensive view of

The White Mountains ranged on either side of the beautiful meadows of the Saco River, with Moat Mount and the Ledges in front on the west, and Kearsarge, Bartlett and Green Hill Range on the east, while Mount Washington can be seen at the head of Intervale on the north, and Cathedral Woods are within easy walking distance.

The House and Furnishings are New and Complete.

Beds furnished with best of Springs and Hair Mattresses.

SUPPLIED WITH PURE MOUNTAIN SPRING WATER.

The Service will be of the best.   Free Carriage to and from depot.

Good Livery connected with the house.

WEEKS & BRUCE, PROPRIETORS.

INTERVALE, N. H.

R. W. WEEKS.   C. J. BRUCE.

Sharing the fate of dozens of White Mountain hotels, the Clarendon was destroyed by fire in December 1962. A motel of the same name still carries on the tradition.

P. O. ADDRESS, INTERVALE, N. H.

❋ ❋ ❋ BELLEVUE HOUSE, ❋ ❋ ❋

NORTH CONWAY, N. H.

JOHN A. BARNES' SONS, - - - PROPRIETORS.

This House accommodates 100 guests, from $2.50 to $3.00 per day for transient, and $9.00 to $15.00 per week, with special rates for June and October. The interior is tasteful, with hardwood floors, easy, handsome staircases, open fireplaces. The location is unsurpassed; the capacity of this House has recently been doubled; pure running water on two floors, and bath-room. The chambers are models of comfort, with beds furnished with woven wire springs and hair mattresses. Its has over 300 feet of broad piazzas, commanding fine views of the Saco, White Mountain Range and neighboring hills. Post and telegraph offices within a few rods of the House. Good Livery in connection. For further particulars address,

J. A. BARNES' SONS, Proprietors.

The Bellevue was built in 1872 and enlarged in 1887. The nearby Clarendon was annexed as part of the Bellevue complex. By 1901, the Bellevue was specializing in winter entertainment, including: sleighing, snowshoeing, camping, coasting, and tobogganing. Skiing had not yet come to the White Mountains.

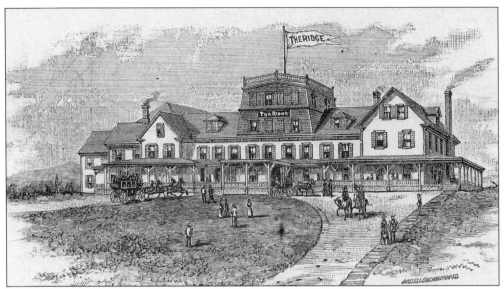

The Ridge in Kearsarge began in 1871 as the Summer House. It was renamed when the Barnes family moved it onto a nearby ridge. The Ridge was destroyed by fire in 1896, rebuilt, and destroyed again in 1905.

This Intervale landmark was built in 1815 by Amos Barnes and was later enlarged by Alonzo Barnes, Amos' son. In 1861 Levi Wheeler bought the inn and renamed it Orient House. Fire leveled the building around 1907.

Three
Wayside Inns

Not all of the White Mountain accommodations were grand hotels. Smaller country inns persisted and flourished. Offering less luxurious environs, the smaller, out-of-the way inns provided an alternative vacation experience.

Many of the wayside hotels were actual working farms, the eastern equivalent of dude ranches. Some became popular with artists and writers seeking a quieter environment in which to work. The tourist economy was stretching into the everyday lives of White Mountain families.

Sam Littlefield's farm, on Bald Hill in Albany, was once a boarding house popular with teachers. Now, greatly enlarged, it is run as the Darby Field Inn.

Guests socialize on the Marshfield House piazza. Note the variety of conveyances shown in this Kilburn Brothers stereograph.

Chisholm's *White Mountain Guide* (1887) waxed poetic about the merits of Fryeburg: "Fryeburg hides its beauties behind deep groves, as the train draws up to the station and the uninstructed traveler would hardly imagine the tranquil delights of this Queen of the Saco Valley, with its deeply shaded streets, bordered by dignified old colonial houses." Ye Old Inn on Main Street is shown here.

The one hundred-guest Chocorua Hotel provided access to the most photographed view in the White Mountains—Chocorua Mountain and Lake. Like many hotels, it ran a farm to provide fresh produce.

The Summer House in Kearsarge Village displays the ubiquitous piazza which was the center of much activity on warm summer days. Some of the larger hotels provided hundreds of feet of verandas. The rockers pictured here were manufactured locally by the thousand and graced the porches of both hotels and private homes.

The .... EDGEWOOD

North Conway
New Hampshire

Among the treats promised by the Edgewood were: mountain climbing, hiking, golf, horseback riding, motoring, bridge, dancing, camera hunting, and picnicking. "From early dawn with its delightful tints of rose and amethyst, to late afternoon, with its golden sunshine and lengthening purple shadows, the [Presidential] range presents an ever changing panorama."

Kezar Lake in Lovell, Maine, offers spectacular mountain views to summer guests. The main lodge at Farringtons was built in 1910 by William and Della Farrington. Tent platforms were later replaced with eighteen cottages. The bucolic nature of the retreat was emphasized by the need to pass through five sheep pasture gates in order to reach the lodge.

454. CHOCORUA INN, CHOCORUA, N.H.

The Chocorua Inn, founded by John Henry Nickerson, was instrumental in luring influential visitors to Chocorua Lake, including the Bowditch family, who saved the lake from being marred by lumbering and development.

It was said of the Elmwood Inn and Cottages in Intervale: "Here they have brought the art of making visitors comfortable and contented to the point of perfection." The same could have been said of almost any White Mountain hostelry; the provision of genteel hospitality was raised to an art form during the grand hotel era.

With large airy rooms, Victorian houses were natural candidates for conversion to inns.

The Summer House, later renamed the Ridge, advertised "Water constantly running through the closets and drains." Because of the problems associated with hotel plumbing, those with good water supplies and adequate drainage made the most of it in their brochures.

Compared to Scottish lochs, Silver Lake was only one of the attractions offered by the Silver Lake House; nearby Madison Boulder and views of Mount Washington also delighted guests. Poet E.E. Cummings spent his summers at a nearby farm.

The descendants of Samuel Thompson, founder of the Kearsarge House, carried on the business on a smaller scale in Kearsarge Hall, part of the family's North Conway Village holdings.

Around 1888, Arthur "El" Wiggin added a wing to each side of the inn formerly run by Charles Purrington. This hotel and restaurant, located near the Barnstormers Theater, now operates as the Tamworth Inn.

The Piper House in Albany was situated at the foot of the Piper Trail, which ascends Mount Chocorua. It was, at various times, known as Wing's Tavern and Clement's Inn. Fire destroyed the venerable building in 1940.

Private stables for guests who brought their own teams were offered by the Alpine in Bethlehem. In 1902, the Alpine advertised "A commodious and elegant new parlor" as part of its improvements.

J.F. Phillips ran the Mountain View House, which was a typical example of Fryeburg's stately colonial homes.

The Woodlawn was located in Fryeburg on what is now called Woodlawn Street. While the inn was in existence, the street was known as Corn Shop Road because of the corn canning plant located there.

Four
New Heights

As the mountains provided motivation to the pioneers of the hotel industry, the mountain peaks supplied the ultimate inspiration, the essence of the White Mountain experience. The Crawfords, realizing the potential draw of Mount Washington, completed a path to the summit in 1819. Ethan Crawford's stone cabin was the forerunner of the summit house-building boom. Monuments to back-breaking labor, the peak houses succumbed, one by one, to the vagaries of nature.

Completed in 1861, the Carriage Road opened Mount Washington to wheeled traffic. Mountain wagons drawn by six strong "roadsters" carried visitors to the summit. The original plan called for the continuation of the road down the other side of the mountain. The first horseless carriage to ascend the mountain was a 6 horsepower, steam-driven Locomobile. This forerunner of the Stanley Steamer was maneuvered up the steep grade in 1899 by inventor Freeland O. Stanley and his wife.

By 1856 the Mount Washington Carriage Road had reached the halfway mark. The road was not completed until 1861, when George W. Lane drove from the Fabyan House stables to the summit.

WHITE MOUNTAINS, N.H., THE HALF-WAY HOUSE,
66022(A)   MT. WASHINGTON CARRIAGE ROAD.

Bradford Washburn, speaking of his 1928 ascent of Mount Washington, described the interior of the Halfway House: "From the front room we went on through a low doorway into a room on the exposed side of the house. This, too, was pitch dark and fearfully cold. There was a small stove in the middle of the floor with a few frost-covered pieces of kindling in front of it. Another little hole of a room appeared before us . . . Two very damp mattresses lay on the floor and a thoroughly rusted bedstead leaned against the wall."

Since Darby Field made his epic ascent in 1632, Mount Washington has attracted and fascinated the bold and the curious. By 1880, ten thousand people were visiting the summit each year. Today the mountain is home to an eclectic colony of weather observers and technicians.

Like most mountaintop buildings, the Mount Washington Stage Office was secured by cables to hold it down in high winds.

Beginning an energetic era of mountaintop building, Ethan Allen Crawford built a stone cabin on the summit of Mount Washington in 1823. The first Tiptop House, built in 1853, was a low, flat structure with an upper promenade. Materials used in the construction of the 28-by-84-foot hotel were transported to the summit on the backs of men and horses. The Tiptop was remodeled in 1862 to its present form.

The Tiptop House survived the 1908 fire that destroyed the second Summit House, but was gutted by flames in 1915. Wind direction was the only factor that saved the newly-rebuilt Summit House from sharing the fate of her sister hotel. The Tiptop was rebuilt with a stone passageway leading to the Summit House.

Mount Washington's famed Tiptop House is considered to be the oldest mountaintop hotel in America. In 1877, a newspaper, appropriately named *Among the Clouds*, began publication in the rear section of the Tiptop.

The Tiptop House has recently been restored as a mountaintop museum. The original moss-covered bunks and cotton partitions have been recreated. (A 1915 newspaper described the interior as containing wooden partitions.)

Utilizing native stone, the earliest Mount Washington Summit House was built in 1852, just to the north of the present Summit House. The second Summit House was built during the summers of 1872 and 1873, but was destroyed by fire in 1908.

The last Summit House, completed in 1915, was equipped with a 100-horsepower Almey water-tube boiler and a Webster Star vacuum water heater. The lighting was supplied by a 7-kilowatt generator connected to a marine-type engine. Newspapers lavished much space on lists of guests at the Summit House and many of the other hostelries. The last Summit House was demolished in 1980.

Horses and carriages were left at the Chocorua Halfway House and those wishing to ascend to the hotel and summit were obliged to continue on foot.

David Knowles, a Silver Lake businessman, conceived and built the Chocorua Peak House. The first shelter, built by Jim Liberty, consisted of a stone foundation covered with a canvas roof. Knowles constructed a larger wooden building on the site. Groceries for the hotel were ordered via a phone line strung from Silver Lake to the summit. A horse named Gypsy was sent unaccompanied to Silver Lake, loaded with supplies, and sent back up the mountain. The first floor contained a kitchen, dining room, and parlor complete with organ for evening entertainment. The second floor housed bedrooms, and there was a dormitory on the third floor. It took four horses to carry the cook stove up the mountain.

In September 1915, Albany resident Ina Morrill was hanging out laundry when she noticed the Chocorua Peak House was missing. In spite of heavy anchor chains, high winds had completely destroyed the two-and-one-half-story hotel. Debris was scattered over a wide area of the summit. The building had not been used as a hotel that summer, but the owner's family had stayed there a few days before its destruction.

The first Kearsarge Peak House is shown here in an early stereograph. Built in 1845, the "Tip Top House" could be reached by bridal path. The Kearsarge Railway Corporation was formed in 1885, but plans to build a railway to the summit were never realized.

After high winds blew apart the first Kearsarge Peak House in 1883, Andrew Dinsmore used the debris to build a smaller facility. The same storm leveled many acres of timber and was responsible for the name of nearby Hurricane Mountain. The second building fulfilled a covenant in the deed requiring that the original structure be replaced within a year. When the second building was destroyed by wind, it was replaced with a fire-watch tower.

Each year, 145,000 vehicles ascend the Mount Washington Auto Road. A large number of these are stages chauffeured by Auto Road staff members. The 7.6-mile road includes grades in excess of 12 percent. During the winter months, Arctic Cats ferry summit workers up the mountain each Wednesday.

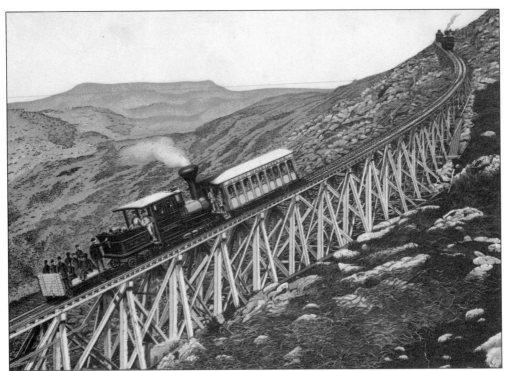

The problems of building a mountain railroad were legion. Jacob's Ladder, one of the many stunning components of the Cog Railway system, is 300 feet long and 30 feet high, with a 36-percent grade.

Although other summit houses became victims of wind, the buildings on the summit of Mount Washington, home of the highest recorded winds on earth, succumbed, not to wind, but to flame. Most notably, a 1908 fire leveled all except the Tiptop House and two stables. When not in flames themselves, mountain peaks were logical places to erect fire-watch stations like this one on Mount Chocorua.

Five

Up from Ashes

The most dreaded word ever uttered in any hotel is "fire." Most White Mountain towns did not have organized fire departments until the twentieth century. Water mains were not installed until the end of the nineteenth century. If a hotel containing several hundred rooms caught fire, little could be done except to save whatever furnishings could be salvaged and to try to keep the blaze from spreading to adjacent buildings.

The hotels burned with regularity. So lucrative was the tourist industry that they rose again and again from the ashes. Usually the replacement was larger than that which had been destroyed. It is remarkable that no building was ever renamed "Phoenix."

Flames leap upward as another of the grand hotels disappears from the landscape.

In 1864, Moses Randall bought a boarding house in North Conway and christened it the Randall House. It was enlarged several times over the next three decades and the Randall family soon developed a reputation for fine cuisine and first-class hospitality. The business was later carried on by Moses' great-great-grandson, Henry Harrison Randall. The first Randall House burned in 1902. Miss Goodwin, a boarder in the hotel, heard the fire crackling and thought a mouse was gnawing on the woodwork. Turning on the light, she discovered smoke rising though cracks in the floor. Although some guests were forced to jump from second and third-floor windows, no one was injured in the conflagration. Only the piano and other parlor furniture were saved.

This 1875 photograph shows the Randall family and guests.

Hotel Randall—North Conway N.H.

Harry Randall was not of a character to be defeated by adversity. The second Hotel Randall was completed in 1903. This three-story, fifty-room inn was touted as state of the art in every respect. The building included ten plate glass "scenery windows" and cypress-paneled sleeping rooms with electric bells. The house was lit throughout by electric lights and boasted modern steam heat. A 35-by-75-foot ell housed the dining room.

The third Hotel Randall was begun in 1925, one month after fire destroyed its predecessor. Containing ninety sleeping rooms, the new hotel boasted fire stops in every wall and a complete sprinkler system. "Vapor" heating allowed the building to stay open throughout the year. In 1926 the building was bought by renowned businessman Harvey Dow Gibson, and renamed the Eastern Slope Inn. Still a familiar North Conway landmark, the third Hotel Randall (the Eastern Slope Inn) continues the hotel tradition in the form of a time-share resort.

Built by John Bellows, the first Glen House (1852–1884) served as a base lodge for those wanting to ascend Mount Washington. The hotel was enlarged in 1865. At least two mountain wagons carried visitors to the summit each day. A favorite trip led tourists up the Cog Railway and then down the other side of the mountain by carriage.

The second Glen House was finished one year after fire destroyed the original building. The new three-story, English Cottage-style hotel provided a 450-foot verandah. In 1893 it, too, was destroyed by fire. In 1901, Charles Milliken converted the servants' quarters into a scaled-down hotel which evaded flames until 1924. The next Glen House, built on the ruins of the servants' quarters, burned in 1967.

Major Samuel Osgood built the first Oxford House in 1775. This early Fryeburg tavern was replaced by a larger inn in 1800. The first Oxford House fire raged through the building in 1887. By 1894, another hotel had risen from the ashes, but in 1906 this structure met the same fate as its predecessor, when a fire originating in the hotel's attic devastated Fryeburg's Main Street. Two nearby residences were dynamited in a vain attempt to alter the fire's course, but flames leapt over the debris and continued their course of destruction. A fire company from Portland arrived only to find that their hoses would not fit the Fryeburg hydrants. In the end, the fire wiped out nearly one-eighth of the town's evaluation.

Among the many owners of the ill-fated Oxford House was Maine Secretary of State Phillip Johnson, father of well-known artist Eastman Johnson. Captain Isaac Frye, grandson of Fryeburg grantee Joseph Frye, also took a turn at running the hotel. Other proprietors bore venerable Fryeburg names like Pike, Boothby, Osgood, Plummer, Knight, and Hastings. Daniel Webster was a boarder at the Oxford during his tenure at Fryeburg Academy.

Carrying on a tradition that spans more than two centuries, a bed and breakfast was opened on this site during the 1980s. The inn, once a private residence, is appropriately named the Oxford House.

Gray's Inn in Jackson was a true phoenix of the grand hotel era. In 1902, fire devastated the original inn. The second inn burned before its completion. A third hotel perished in January 1916. The fourth Gray's Inn persevered in a decayed state until 1983 when, again, the flames took their toll.

The Sunset Pavilion in North Conway had been annexed to the nearby Eastern Slope Inn when local pilot Wylie Apte noticed smoke rising from the roof. Unable to attract attention to the fire by dipping his wings, he flew to the White Mountain Airport to report the blaze.

Birchmont, located on Sunset Hill in North Conway, was built as a vacation home for Maine Central Railroad President Payson Tucker. A special spur was built to allow Mr. and Mrs. Tucker and their guests to arrive by private railway car. Businessman Harvey Dow Gibson acquired the property as a retreat for executives from the Manufacturers' Trust, where he served as president.

Under the ownership of Louisa Jones, Birchmont flew the Texas flag. It was later operated as an inn until 1970, when fire leveled the historic structure. The site is now occupied by the 152-room Red Jacket Mountain View Motor Inn.

Six
Decline and Decay

At first, hotel owners saw the automobile as a new source of revenue. Stables were converted to garages and facilities were built to house chauffeurs. Soon, however, it became apparent that the horseless carriage signaled the end of an era. There was no longer any need to remain for weeks in one spot; America was on the move. A new type of hostelry sprang up: overnight cabins began to dot the countryside, followed by motels.

One by one the hotels began to close, empty specters silhouetted against a changing sky. When a hotel burned, it was not rebuilt. The era of the "grand hotel" was at an end.

The automobile gave Americans a freedom they had never known. Day trips to the mountains became possible.

The newly-mobile population demanded and got improved roads. Country lanes, once filled with tallyhos, began to teem with carriages of the horseless kind.

Tourists began to enjoy the open road. Fewer people were content to spend weeks in one place. Travelers needed only a bed for the night. The huge hotels became superfluous.

The automobile was only one factor in the ultimate decline of the hotel era. Changing tastes, changing incomes, and a national restlessness all contributed to an atmosphere that no longer fostered the grand hotel mentality.

GATEWAY – MOTEL AND COTTAGES

CONWAY
NEW HAMPSHIRE

●

½ Mile North
Over Bridge
on Route 16

Inexpensive and plentiful, overnight cabins suited the needs of the new White Mountain tourist. Cabins evolved into motels and a new, universal hostelry was born. The Gateway went through the full cycle, beginning as Ormand Merrill's resort farm, adding cabins and a motel, and later, being renovated as the Merrill Farm Resort.

Once a fine hotel, the Pequawket House in Conway Village lingered on in slow, agonizing decline. It was claimed that Abraham Lincoln had once been a guest of the venerable tavern, but this has never been confirmed.

The last in a series of Gray's Inns in Jackson struggled on for a while as a youth camp under the name Hampshire House. After nearly two decades of disuse, the massive relic of another age inevitably succumbed to fire.

After the hotel business began to decline, the Pequawket House in Conway Village survived for a while as a boarding house for workers from the Conway Lumber Company. Shown above is the bakery owned by John Shorey and Joseph Edwards, one of several businesses that were housed in the building. The Pequawket House was razed in 1923 to make room for Kennett High School.

Samuel Thoms' house, built in 1823, became the main section of the Presidential Inn. The inn opened in 1917 and served as a center of Conway Village social life.

Declining business sounded the death knell of the Presidential Inn. Ending an era in Conway Village, the much-loved landmark was torn down in 1971.

An outlet mall now fills the site once occupied by the stately Presidential Inn.

Hotels were not the only victims of America's new-found mobility. Railroad passenger service slowly declined and eventually disappeared in many areas. In 1960, the Conway Station was dismantled to make way for the Route 16 bypass.

In operation for almost a century, the Twin Mountain House complex included the 110-room main building, dormitory, recreation hall, garage, and maintenance building. Bits and pieces of many of the White Mountain hotels are now scattered across the countryside, salvaged for use in other buildings.

Once overlooking the tent where Reverend Henry Ward Beecher conducted summer services, the Twin Mountain House was dismantled in 1960.

Seven

Renaissance

A few of the hotels survived, were refurbished, and remain in operation today. Many of the inns have taken on renewed vitality because of the recent popularity of bed and breakfasts. Against all odds, a few have remained in constant operation for more than a century. Some forward-thinking individuals have begun to build new facilities in the White Mountains. Perhaps, Americans are again coming under the spell of the "grand hotel."

Surviving depression and bankruptcy, The Balsams is one of the great hotel success stories. Beginning as the Dix House, The Balsams has remained in business since 1866. Expansions during the 1870s and '80s raised the hotel's capacity to one hundred. During World War I, the first multi-story steel frame and masonry structure in New Hampshire was added to the main building.

Defying the odds, the Mount Washington, queen of the grand hotels, has avoided fire and survived famine. Although the hotel has changed ownership several times during the last three decades, its future looks encouraging.

North Conway's Keeley Institute was an inn with an attitude. For several years, under the auspices of Dr. Leslie E. Keeley, Forest Glen Inn was used as a sanatorium for the cure of addiction to alcohol, tobacco, and opium. Spouses of those taking the "Keeley cure" were invited to stay at the facility, which was "More quietly conducted than any summer hotel or boarding place." After the Keeley method went out of fashion, the building resumed operation as an inn, noted for its "Radium Spring" (the owners called it "A true fountain of life"). The alkaline water was advertised as superior to Poland Spring water and "Almost specific for all kidney diseases, and liver and stomach troubles."

The love of horses demonstrated during the lavish coaching parades continued to be demonstrated in the Eastern Slope horse shows of the 1940s. Now the tradition is carried on through the annual Equine Festival.

Originally the summer cottage and farm of carpet heiress Helen Bigelow and her husband, Daniel Merriman, Stonehurst was converted to an inn in 1946.

Under the auspices of Helen Bigelow Merriman, Stonehurst was the social center of the Eastern Slope. As Stonehurst Manor, it continues to serve as a center of elegance and hospitality.

By the 1970s, Wentworth Hall in Jackson was slowly rotting away. Plans to raze it and build vacation chalets were thwarted by zoning regulations. The complex has now been renovated and is once again operating as a resort hotel.

The Eagle Mountain House in Jackson commands fine views of Carter Notch, its impressive lines creating a silhouette from former days. Standing in its shadow, modern sojourners can imagine the grandeur of the past.